FINDING
STRENGTH
IN WEAKNESS

COMPACT EXPOSITORY PULPIT COMMENTARY SERIES

FINDING STRENGTH IN WEAKNESS

Drawing Upon
the Existing Grace Within

DAVID A. HARRELL

© 2020 David A. Harrell

ISBN 978-1-7343452-4-7

Great Writing Publications, 425 Roberts Road, Taylors, SC 29687 www.greatwriting.org

Shepherd's Fire 5245 Highway 41-A Joelton, TN 37080 www.shepherdsfire.com

All Scripture quotations, unless stated otherwise, are taken from the New American Standard Bible® (NASB), Copyright © 1960, 1962, 1963, 1968, 1971, 1972, 1973, 1975, 1977, 1995 by The Lockman Foundation. Used by permission. www.Lockman. org All rights reserved.

No part of this publication may be reproduced, or stored in a retrieval system, or transmitted, in any form or by any means, mechanical, electronic, photocopying, recording or otherwise, without the prior permission of the publishers.

Shepherd's Fire exists to proclaim the unsearchable riches of Christ through mass communications for the teaching ministry of Bible expositor David Harrell, with a special emphasis in encouraging and strengthening pastors and church leaders.

Table of Contents

Books in this Series *6*

Field-Preachers of Uncommon Valor *7*

Weaknesses Exposed *25*

The Teacher *44*

The Soldier *60*

The Athlete *73*

The Farmer *85*

Endnotes *96*

Books in this Series

Finding Grace in Sorrow: Enduring Trials with the Joy of the Holy Spirit

Finding Strength in Weakness: Drawing Upon the Existing Grace Within

Glorifying God in Your Body: Seeing Ourselves from God's Perspective

God, Evil, and Suffering: Understanding God's Role in Tragedies and Atrocities

God's Gracious Gift of Assurance: Rediscovering the Benefits of Justification by Faith

Our Sin and the Savior: Understanding the Need for Renewing and Sanctifying Grace

The Marvel of Being in Christ: Adoring God's Loving Provision of New Life in the Spirit

The Miracle of Spiritual Sight: Affirming the Transforming Doctrine of Regeneration

1

Field-Preachers of Uncommon Valor

> "... My grace is sufficient for you, for power is perfected in weakness" ... Therefore I am well content with weaknesses, with insults, with distresses, with persecutions, with difficulties, for Christ's sake; for when I am weak, then I am strong.
>
> 2 CORINTHIANS 12:9–10

One of the most remarkable books I have ever read was written by a Scottish divine and biographer, William Garden Blaikie, D.D., LL.D. (1820–1899), Professor of Apologetical and of Pastoral Theology, New College, Edinburgh, Scotland. The title of his work is *The Preachers of Scotland from the Sixth to the Nineteenth Century*,[1] a detailed history of how God empowered fearless servants to bring the gospel to the wild barbarians of Scotland, and how that gospel saved and radically changed them. As I was transported to another time and another place, I was deeply impacted by the great mystery of godliness at work in the early days of Scotland when

> . . . missionaries, with tearful eye and trembling lip, told them of the manger of Bethlehem and the cross of Calvary. What else could have dispossessed the old gods from their hearts at a stroke, spite of all they had learned from their fathers? What else could have turned these shaggy men and women, hardly less wild-looking than the cattle of their mountains, into devout and earnest followers of a crucified Jew?[2]

With vivid language and biblical theology—combined with first-source historical accounts from eyewitness testimonies, journals, and some recorded sermons—Blaikie took me on an unforgettable journey to witness the power of God at work in a pagan land. From the earliest days when Roman soldiers in the invading army were "moved by the love of Christ," and "followed it to cast the seed of the Gospel into the furrows of war,"[3] through the great preachers of the Reformation and Covenanting Period of Scotland, his recounting of history caused me to stand in reverential awe as I beheld the agencies of divine providence at work in accomplishing the sovereign purposes of God.

The annals of Scottish religious history repeatedly demonstrated how the power of sound doctrine (decidedly Calvinistic) would prevail over the church's tendency toward compromise, especially in those seasons when it embraced the "doctrines of Pelagianism and Arminianism," that "ultimately developed into deism and indifferentism."[4] But his chronicles of the persecuted Field-Preachers that resulted from the edicts of King Charles II of England were especially moving to me, especially in light of the topic of this mini-book, *Finding Strength in Weakness: Drawing Upon the Existing Grace Within*.

Field-Preachers

During the dreadful years of persecution between 1663 and 1688, young clergymen who championed Presbyterian church polity and a robust Reformed soteriology were driven from their charges, and under the "threat of fine and imprisonment, of torture or of death"[5] were restricted from preaching the only gospel that can save. With no way of earning a living, and with orders from the King to inflict heavy fines, imprisonment, and even torture leading to death upon anyone who helped a them, "the preacher, with a great price on his head, had no certain dwelling-place, and where there was no friendly cottage to shelter him, had to wander about in wild lonely places, sleeping in woods and caves, often cold and wet and hungry; racked by rheumatism or prostrated by dysentery, glad if he could succeed in keeping his pocket-Bible dry."[6]

These great soldiers of the cross were affectionately called, "Field-Preachers"—men of uncommon valor. With gloomy colors Blaikie painted the tragedies and triumphs of those days on a dark canvas of satanic oppression. He writes,

> If ever circumstances compelled the Lord's servants to preach "as dying men to dying men," it was then. Neither preacher nor hearer could ever be sure that the dragoons would not burst on them before the sermon was ended, or that before nightfall their life-blood would not be staining the ground. . . . Preachers seemed at times to feel the bloody rope round their neck, or the bullet in their brain; the word came from their hearts and went to the hearts of their hearers, and stuck there for their conversion, confirmation, and

comfort. Persecution, like the deathbed, has a wonderful sifting power. It tears away all disguises, shams, falsehoods, and formalities; it compels men to look the stern realities of life and death right in the face, it sweeps away the refuges of lies, and leaves only those truths to cling to which will sustain them in the agony of conflict.[7]

Despite the satanic onslaught of persecution designed to terrorize both the Field-Preachers and those who would hear them with the threat of imprisonment and death—often a slow and agonizing death—these men proclaimed the unsearchable riches of Christ with fervent boldness. Their sermons thundered across the moors and mountain recesses of the northern third of the island of Great Britain, often to massive crowds who were hungry for the great saving, liberating, and transforming truths of the gospel.

Richard Cameron

One such Field-Preacher was a young man named Richard Cameron (1648?–22 July 1680); a man who refused to submit to the Crown's High Church Anglican form of church governance (episcopacy) that sought to control the Church of Scotland through their appointed (apostate) bishops and demanded that the King be considered the head of the church (rather than Christ). Refusing to submit to such an unbiblical ecclesiology with its concomitant heresies, Cameron became a leader of the militant Presbyterians known as the Covenanters.

A born preacher with no formal theological training apart from what he received from other field-preachers, he was a mighty and fearless preacher in the spirit of the apostles. In his book, *The Scottish Covenanters: 1638–88*, James Dodds (1813–1874) paints a beautiful picture of the Spirit-empowered revivals that marked those days; a season when thousands of saints and sinners met in the wilderness to worship God by hearing Cameron preach the gospel while other men stood guard in the distance. Here's a description of such a scene:

> Picture to yourselves this noble and majestic youth, with blooming countenance and eagle eye, standing on some huge rock uplifted in the wilderness. Ten thousand people are grouped around him: the aged, with the women and children, seated near this pulpit of nature's handiwork; the men of middle age and the stalwart youths of the surround-

ing hamlets composing the outer circle, many of them with their hands on their swords, or their trusty guns slung by their side; and on each neighbouring height may be seen the solitary figure of the watchman, intently gazing in all directions for the approach of the troopers who are now kept garrisoned in every district, and who night and day are on the prowl to catch some poor outlawed Covenanter, or surprise some conventicle in the depths of the hills. It is a Sabbath in May. The great wild moor stretches out to a kind of infinity, blending at last with the serene blue sky. How sublime and peaceful the moment! Even in this age of violence and oppression—of the dungeon, the rack, and the scaffold, and murder in cold blood in the fields. Heaven smiles on the "remnant." All is hushed and reverent in attention. The word is precious. . . . The psalm has been sung, and the echoes of the myriad voices have died on the moorland breeze. The prayer has been offered, the earnest wrestlings with Heaven of men who before sunset may themselves be an offering for their religion. The preacher rises. He eyes for a moment in silence that vast multitude, gathered from all parts of the West. Always serious, always inspired with elevated feeling, there is in his manner more than the usual solemnity. . . . Yes, he knows that his days are numbered; and but a few more suns the heather sod shall be his bed of death. A strange, almost unearthly sympathy is visible, stirring those assembled thousands to the very depths of their being. Rousing himself from the reverie which had passed over him, the preacher announces his text—"Ye will not come to me that ye might have life."[8]

My purpose here is simple: I wish to give you a glimpse of a man—like many others—who knew what it was to *find strength in weakness*. Young Cameron knew how to tap into the resources that were his because of his union with Christ—a foreign concept to many Christians. He understood and applied Paul's admonition to Timothy when he said, "You therefore, my son, be strong in the grace that is in Christ Jesus. . . . Suffer hardship with me, as a good soldier of Christ Jesus" (2 Tim. 2:1, 3). And suffer he did.

On 22 July, government dragoons killed Cameron at Airds Moss near Cumnock. There they mutilated his body by severing his hands and head from it. Then, in perhaps a more heinous act of barbaric cruelty, they took his head and hands to Edinburgh to show to his father who was incarcerated there for the same crimes. It is hard to imagine a more macabre scene, or fathom a more satanic hatred capable of evoking such evil in the hearts of men. When the father was asked if he recognized the hands and head he responded, "I know them. I know them. They are my son's, my own dear son's. It is the Lord. Good is the will of the Lord, who cannot wrong me or mine, but has made goodness and mercy to follow us all our days."[9] His head was then placed upon a pole and paraded through the streets of Edinburgh. His hands and his head were finally affixed to the Nether-Bow Gate for public display.[10]

Elusive Spiritual Strength

When considering the violent opposition to the truth that has marked not only the history of Scotland, but countless other countries, any reasonable person must admit that something supernatural is at work. Something so sinister, so evil, so powerful, that it can only be described as satanic. Truly we "wrestle not against flesh and blood, but against the rulers, against the powers, against the world forces of this darkness, against the spiritual forces of wickedness in the heavenly places" (Eph. 6:12); requiring every Christian to "be strong in the Lord, and in the strength of His might" (v. 10), like Richard Cameron and thousands of others like him down through redemptive history.

Jesus warned us that the world would always hate those who belong to Him "because you are not of the world, but I chose you out of the world, because of this the world hates you" (John 15:19). From the days of the Old Testament prophets through the New Testament era of Christ and the apostles, divinely appointed men who have proclaimed the truths of God's revelation have been violently opposed, imprisoned, tortured, and killed—our sinless Savior being the supreme example. *Foxe's Book of Martyrs* provides numerous examples of men and women during the time of the Reformation that took a stand against the religious abuses that had taken over the church. Untold numbers of godly men and women who embraced the true gospel were so hated by the forces of evil that they were forced to pay for their faith with their very lives.

This has been, and will continue to be, the history of the church until Christ returns. The fact that throughout history New Testament Christianity has been hated (unlike the numerous counterfeits that have always existed) is not strange to those who belong to Christ. They understand their citizenship is in heaven (Phil. 3:20) and they are therefore content in being "aliens and strangers" (1 Peter 2:11) in a world of which they have no part (John 15:19). But this doesn't make it any easier when it comes to doing battle with sin—theirs and others'. Although we know "that the sufferings of this present time are not worthy to be compared with the glory that is to be revealed to us" (Rom. 8:18), we still "groan within ourselves, waiting eagerly for *our* adoption as sons, the redemption of our body" (v. 23) when, in our glorification, we finally and fully enter into the ineffable splendor of our inheritance. Even our Lord was "despised and forsaken of men, a man of sorrows and acquainted with grief" (Isa. 53:3) and was so overcome by the prospect of the cross that an angel was sent to strengthen him in the garden of Gethsemane (Luke 22:43).

Though the agonies of Christ were infinitely greater than anything we would ever even imagine much less endure, we are all prone to debilitating physical and spiritual weakness. But knowing how to find spiritual strength in those seasons of weakness—especially in the face of persecution—is elusive for most. Unfortunately, far too often men and women who have demonstrated remarkable strength of character and resolute faith in the midst of some great trial are considered to be the recipients of supernatural resources unavailable to the average Christian and therefore unattainable to most. But such is not the case. Every believer united to Christ in saving faith possesses all that is His—what Paul described as "the surpassing greatness of His power toward us who believe. . . . in accordance with the working of the strength of His might which He brought about in Christ" (Eph. 1:19–20).

Spirit Filling

To be sure, the debilitating problems of life can exhaust even the most devout Christian—even as it weakened the resolve of the apostle Paul himself (2 Cor. 2:12). We all need a supernatural dose of spiritual strength. Unfortunately, however, spiritual limitations and failures can be fertile soil for the seeds of charismatic error to be planted. Self–promoting charlatans tell naïve and gullible people seeking divine power that they need to be "filled with the Spirit," which typically leads to the practice of being "slain in the Spirit." They insist that this will produce a "Spirit-filled Christian" (in contrast to a non-Spirit-filled Christian which is no Christian at all [Rom. 8:9]). Evidence of such a phenomenon will, according to them, result in the gift of speaking in tongues, which in reality is nothing more than a nonsensical counterfeit of the true gift of languages described in the New Testament (see Acts 2:6–11). Other bizarre behaviors that supposedly result from this supernatural empowerment include things like falling to the floor, laughing uncontrollably, barking like a dog, erratic shaking, and staggering around as if in a drunken stupor. In fact, no conduct—no matter how absurd or irrational—is considered unacceptable.

What they fail to understand—and what every believer should cherish—is that the very moment God's Spirit imparts eternal life to the spiritually dead in regeneration (Eph. 2:1–3), multiple supernatural transactions involving the Holy Spirit occur simultaneously:

- Christ *baptizes* the believer with the Spirit into the body of Christ (1 Cor. 12:13).
- The Father *seals* the believer with the Holy Spirit as a show of ownership and a guarantee of one's salvation (Eph. 1:13).
- The Spirit *indwells* the believer (1 Cor. 3:16).
- The Spirit *fills/controls* the believer (Eph. 5:18).
- The Spirit *produces* spiritual fruit in the believer's life (Gal. 5:22–23).
- The Spirit *gifts* the believer for service in the church (1 Cor. 12:4).[11]

Furthermore, at the moment of salvation, we are forever united to Christ. For we have been *crucified* with him (Gal. 2:20), we have *died* with him (Rom. 6:8; Col. 2:20), we have been *buried* with him (Rom. 6:3), we have been *raised* up with him to walk in newness of life (Eph. 2:5–6; Rom. 6:4), and we have been *seated* with Him in the heavenly places (Eph. 2:6).

Christ is no longer *outside* us; He dwells *within* us, and *we* in Him, for indeed, we are a branch attached to the vine that is Christ. And solely because of His power we are able to bear spiritual fruit (John 15:5). Indeed, the "Father of our Lord Jesus Christ. . . has blessed us with every spiritual blessing in the heavenly places in Christ" (Eph. 1:3). We are "a temple of the living God" (2 Cor. 6:16); "His divine power has granted to us everything pertaining to life and godliness" (2 Peter 1:3), and we now "[strive] according to His power, which mightily works within [us]" (Col. 1:29). We are forever united to the One who "is able to do exceeding abundantly beyond all that we ask or think, according to the power that works within us"(Eph. 3:20).

Accessing Resources We Already Possess

But practically speaking, many Christians wonder how they can access the resources they already possess in Christ. Asked simply, *How can we find strength in weakness*? This is truly an elusive aspiration for many believers. Routinely I talk with discouraged, disappointed, defeated, even depressed Christians who feel they are powerless, ineffective, unproductive, useless, and terrified to take a stand for Christ. Because of the inevitable sorrows of life and the contempt of this world they feel powerless. They respond to the admonition to "be strong in the Lord" by saying, "Yeah, right!" They hear someone say, "I can do all things through Christ who strengthens me" and they reply, "Not me." They hear stories of the Richard Camerons of the world and think to themselves, "Whatever he had, I don't have it."

Most are clueless as to how the apostle Paul could refuse to glory in his strengths, as most of us do, but instead, *gloried in his weaknesses*! And like all of us, Paul had his weaknesses. Evidently he was not a very impressive man to look at or to listen to. According to his critics, "his personal presence [was] unimpressive and his speech contemptible" (2 Cor. 10:10). How would you like to have that reputation spread all over social media? He even admitted that he was "unskilled in speech" (2 Cor. 11:6). Add to this all the physical sufferings he endured over the course of his ministry (2 Cor. 11:23), and you have to wonder how he could have ever survived, much less thrived in his service to Christ. Yet still he said, "If I have to boast, I will boast of what pertains to my weakness" (v. 29).

Then, as if all that wasn't enough to break him, to counterbalance the gravity of his trip to the third heaven, God afflicted him with "a thorn in the flesh" that he described as "a messenger of Satan to buffet me... to keep me from exalting myself" (2 Cor. 12:7). As anyone would do, he petitioned three times for the Lord to remove the thorn, but His request was denied. But instead of moping around aimlessly in despair like Eeyore (the lugubrious, pessimistic, depressed little donkey in Winnie-the-Pooh), he actually found strength in his weakness! Why? How? Because he knew Christ would be a more glorious compensation! He knew Christ was able to empower him in ways he could have never imagined as a result of his affliction. In light of this the Lord said to him,

> "My grace is sufficient for you, for power is perfected in weakness," to which Paul responded, "Most gladly, therefore I will rather boast about my weaknesses, that the power of Christ may dwell in me. Therefore I am well content with weaknesses, with insults, with

distresses, with persecutions, with difficulties, for Christ's sake; for when I am weak, then I am strong" (vv. 9–10).

Commenting on this, Maurice Roberts offers a very practical analysis that is sure to bring conviction to every believer who is not already hopelessly biased in his own favor:

> Is it not here at this very point that Paul was so strong and many are so weak? "The Power of Christ"! What is that, but the power of Christ's grace to sweeten life, to sanctify affliction, to purify the soul, to brighten our hopes, to gladden our hearts and even to give unction to our preaching? Here is the needed dimension! But so long as the church glories in itself, we forfeit this blessing. To project our 'better side' for all the world to see, is to drive out the abiding presence of Christ. . . . The conclusion seems inescapable. The way to grow in strength is to diminish in self-importance. The way to enjoy more of Christ in our lives is to be more honest, more realistic about what we are and less obsessed with the urge to keep up appearances with other people at all costs.[12]

Knowing our weaknesses is one thing, but admitting them is another thing altogether. But even then, being able to find strength when life gets really brutal can seem impossible. Timothy—the apostle Paul's son in the faith—struggled with this very thing. And as we will see, God revealed to him some very practical ways to tap into the resources he already possessed, bringing him much-needed comfort and encouragement, while at the same time giving him power to persevere and prevail in the face of overwhelming forces of opposition. And to these great truths we now turn our attention.

2

Weaknesses Exposed

You therefore, my son, be strong in the grace that is in Christ Jesus.
2 TIMOTHY 2:1

The Bible describes many men and women who struggled with various forms of weakness in faith and character. And without fail when they yielded to some form of temptation and committed some act of disobedience, they would end up experiencing all manner of divine chastening. If we're honest with ourselves, we can all identify with their defective qualities in one way or another, and in some cases we may have even experienced similar kinds of disturbing outcomes.

For example, twice in a season of FEAR Abram's faith in God grew weak, causing him to take matters into his own hands and lie about Sarai being his wife (Gen. 12:13; 20:1). In a season of BARRENNESS, IMPATIENCE, and DOUBT in the promises of God, Sarai hatched a plot to gain an heir by giving a concubine slave to her husband resulting in the birth of Ishmael (Gen. 16:1–6). In a season of SELF-WILLED DISOBEDIENCE, Isaac ignored the promise of God to his wife Rebecca (that the older twin would serve the younger [Gen. 25:23]), and planned to grant his eldest son Esau the blessing of birthright—despite his grievous marriages (26:35). In a season of FRUSTRATION when the children of Israel contended with Moses over a lack of water, Moses failed to take God at His word and treat Him as holy before the people. In anger he *struck* the designated rock to produce water rather than *speaking* to it (Gen. 20:7–12). In a season of MORAL LAXITY, David was overpowered by the lust of his flesh when he gazed upon a beautiful woman and not only committed adultery with her, but indirectly murdered her husband (2 Sam. 11:1–21). In a season of SPIRITUAL OVERCONFIDENCE, Peter yielded to the fear of man and denied the Lord three times (Matt. 26:69–74). In each scenario of spiritual weakness, the consequence of disobedience was dire.

The Danger of Weakening Spiritually

While many other Old and New Testament examples could be cited, I want to focus on a young man who was truly the epitome of weakness and in need of much exhortation, encouragement, and practical instruction. I'm referring to a young pastor named Timothy, the apostle Paul's son in the faith.

As we read the New Testament record concerning him, we can safely conclude that Timothy was weak physically, spiritually, and emotionally; a timid young man who, according to the wise purposes of God, was thrust into leadership at the church at Ephesus (founded by the apostle Paul). But Paul's epistles to him (1 and 2 Timothy) make it clear that he struggled with *personal problems, pastoral pressures,* and the *mounting persecution of the world*. Even a cursory perusal of Paul's exhortations to him demonstrates the severity and scope of his weaknesses.

- Have nothing to do with worldly fables fit only for old women. On the other hand, discipline yourself for the purpose of godliness (1 Tim. 4:7).
- Let no one look down on your youthfulness, but *rather* in speech, conduct, love, faith *and* purity, show yourself an example of those who

believe. . . . give attention to the public reading of Scripture, to exhortation and teaching. Do not neglect the spiritual gift within you. . . . Take pains with these things; be absorbed in them. . . . Pay close attention to yourself and to your teaching; persevere in these things, for as you do this you will ensure salvation both for yourself and for those who hear you (1 Tim. 4:12–16).
- Flee from these things [the love of money], you man of God, and pursue righteousness, godliness, faith, love, perseverance *and* gentleness. Fight the good fight of faith; take hold of the eternal life to which you were called, and you made the good confession in the presence of many witnesses. I charge you in the presence of God . . . that you keep the commandment without stain or reproach until the appearing of our Lord Jesus Christ (1 Tim. 6:11–14).
- Kindle afresh the gift of God which is in you. . . for God has not given us a spirit of timidity, but of power and love and discipline (2 Tim. 1:6–7).
- Do not be ashamed of the testimony of our Lord" (v. 8). . . for this reason I also suffer these things, but I am not ashamed; for I know

whom I have believed and I am convinced that He is able to guard what I have entrusted to Him until that day (v. 12).

- Retain the standard of sound words which you have heard from me. . . . Guard, through the Holy Spirit who dwells in us, the treasure which has been entrusted to you (vv. 13–14).
- Be strong in the grace that is in Christ Jesus. The things which you have heard from me in the presence of many witnesses, entrust these to faithful men. . . . Suffer hardship with me, as a good soldier of Christ Jesus (2:1–4).
- Be diligent to present yourself approved to God as a workman who does not need to be ashamed, accurately handling the word of truth. But avoid worldly and empty chatter, for it will lead to further ungodliness (vv. 15–16).
- I solemnly charge *you*. . . preach the word; be ready in season and out of season; reprove, rebuke, exhort, with great patience and instruction (4:1–2).
- Be sober in all things, endure hardship, do the work of an evangelist, fulfill your ministry (v. 5).

Combating the Wolves

It's obvious that Timothy lacked the strength of character necessary to keep the wolves at bay. As in the case of most churches today, some arrogant and aggressive heretics had gained a platform in the church, causing some of the members to defect from sound doctrine. Paul exposed them publicly. He called them by name: "Hymenaeus and Alexander, whom I have delivered to Satan, so that they may be taught not to blaspheme" (1 Tim. 1:20); and Philetus (2 Tim. 2:17), who was Alexander's replacement and Hymenaeus' accomplice. They were all factious heretics—men known for their "worldly and empty chatter" that "[led] to further ungodliness" and whose "talk. . . spread like gangrene. . . men who have gone astray from the truth" and "upset the faith of some" (2 Tim. 2:16–18).

Naturally, this was of great concern for Paul. In fact, at the close of his first letter he writes: "O Timothy, guard what has been entrusted to you, avoiding worldly and empty chatter and the opposing arguments of what is falsely called "knowledge"—which some have professed and thus gone astray from the faith" (1 Tim. 6:20–21). Any man who has ever served in pastoral ministry knows how personally devastating and distracting it is to have to deal with heretics. No wonder Paul exhorts us to deal with them swiftly and decisively (Rom. 16:17; 2 Thess. 3:14–15; Titus 3:10; 2 Tim. 2:25). This was a lesson Timothy had to learn as well.

Mounting Persecution of the World

Worse yet, the wicked, Christian-hating emperor Nero was escalating his persecution against the saints in the Roman Empire. In fact, Paul wrote 2 Timothy while shackled in chains (2:9) in a damp, cold prison cell (4:13) knowing he would never be released (4:6) and fully aware that his execution was imminent, having been charged as a criminal against the empire. According to tradition, he suffered the martyrdom he had envisioned in 4:6: "For I am already being poured out as a drink offering, and the time of my departure has come" (4:6). For this reason, Paul summoned Timothy, urging him to come quickly to visit him one last time (4:9, 21); although there's no record of whether he did or didn't.

With Nero's persecution intensifying, many Christians were afraid, including Timothy. All of Paul's close companions in ministry—except Luke (4:11) and Onesiphorus and his household—had abandoned him for fear of persecution (*cf.* 1:15; 4:9–12, 16). Naturally, Paul was afraid that timid Timothy would also collapse under the combined weight of church troublemakers and Nero's satanically empowered rage against Christians.

Put yourself in Timothy's position. How would you feel if you knew there was a good possibility that you might be on Nero's hit list? Moreover, imagine being one of the terrified saints of that day. Think how you would feel if some of the wicked political groups that exist in our government actually seized full control of our government and ultimately outlawed biblical Christianity? What if they said to you, "Renounce your faith in Christ or go to prison or be killed?"

The devastating fire in Rome (July of AD 64) was blamed on Christians, the convenient scapegoat Nero used to cover up his own wickedness. It's important to note that Paul wrote 2 Timothy around AD 66–67, and Nero began his persecution in AD 67. The fire in Rome also ignited government-sponsored persecution where Christians were arrested, tortured, fed to wild beasts, crucified, and even made to wear garments made stiff with tar so they could be set ablaze and used as torches to light the sadistic Nero's gardens.

In *The Annals* of Tacitus, written by Cornelius Tacitus (c. AD 56 – c. 120)—a Roman historian and senator—Tacitus describes Nero's treatment of Christians as follows:

Therefore, first those were seized who admitted their faith, and then, using the information they provided, a vast multitude [of Christians] were convicted, not so much for the crime of burning the city, but for hatred of the human race. And perishing they were additionally made into sports: they were killed by dogs by having the hides of beasts attached to them, or they were nailed to crosses or set aflame, and, when the daylight passed away, they were used as nighttime lamps.[13]

The world's hatred of Christians continued in the second and third centuries, especially in the Roman Empire, reaching its zenith in the fourth century under the savage rule of Diocletian who attempted to exterminate Christianity altogether. This continued until the rule of Constantine who claimed to convert to Christianity and who put a temporary end to the persecution in the proclamation of the Edict of Milan, which decreed tolerance for Christianity in the Empire.

But this always has been, and will continue to be the cross the church must bear until Christ returns. Theologian, John MacArthur captures this when he says:

Under the Roman Catholic Church, which replaced Imperial Rome as the dominant power during the Middle Ages, persecution broke out anew. Ironically, this time the persecution against true believers came from those who called themselves "Christian." The horrors of the Inquisition, the St. Bartholomew's Day Massacre, and the martyrdoms of many believers epitomized the Roman Church's effort to suppress the true gospel of Jesus Christ. More recently, believers have been brutally repressed by Communist and Islamic regimes. In fact, it has been estimated by none other than a Roman Catholic source that, in all of church history, roughly 70 million Christians have been killed for their profession of faith, with two-thirds of those martyrdoms occurring in or after the start of the twentieth century. The actual number is likely much greater. The Catholic journalist cited in this news article estimates that an average of 100,000 Christians have been killed every year since 1990.[14]

Today in America it is politically correct to demean Bible-believing Christians. We're increasingly maligned and marginalized, and typically depicted as ignorant, hypocritical, narrow-minded bigots by the Hollywood and media elites. I don't think I have to convince any believer that the world's hatred of true, biblical Christianity is alive and well, and even on the increase around the globe. I shudder to think what our children will face when they become adults, if the Lord tarries.

Paul's Concern

Obviously, first-century saints lived in a perilous season that would test the mettle of anyone's character—a very difficult time for Paul to pass the non-apostolic mantle of ministry to Timothy (2 Tim. 2:2). Knowing he was about to die, and knowing Timothy's spiritual knees were knocking together in fear, Paul was legitimately concerned. It is reasonable to assume that people were leaving the church in Ephesus like some had abandoned Paul who said: "All who are in Asia turned away from me, among whom are Phygelus and Hermogenes" (2 Tim. 2:15)—a desertion that would have undoubtedly brought him great disappointment. Timothy would have probably known these two men as well. It would be safe to assume that some of Timothy's friends were abandoning him, too. So Paul is thinking, "Who's going to carry on the work of the ministry if Timothy fails?"

God knew that His servant Timothy needed help. He needed to be strengthened in his resolve to trust and obey, as we all do. He needed to know how to find strength in weakness. So under the inspiration of the Spirit, Paul admonished him, saying, "You therefore, my son, be strong in the grace that is in Christ Jesus" (2 Tim. 2:1). Essentially he's saying, "You have no strength in yourself, but you have unlimited, supernatural strength in the grace that is in Christ Jesus."

Think of "grace" in this context as *the sufficiency of Christ to whom we are united*. Jesus described this in John 15:5 where He says: "I am the vine, you are the branches; he who abides in Me, and I in him, he bears much fruit; for apart from Me you can do nothing." To "abide" means to remain or continue—which is the obvious result of being united to Christ. Jesus stated this clearly when he said, "you in me, and I in you" (14:20). Practically speaking, to *"abide in Christ"* means to remain in fellowship with God in Christ—to have a sustained conscious communion with Him—because sometimes that fellowship is interrupted by sin. Paul exhorted the Ephesians, in this regard, saying, "Do not be foolish, but understand what the will of the Lord is. And do not get drunk with wine. . . but be filled with the Spirit" (Eph. 5:15–

16). This is the same as walking in the Spirit (Gal. 5:15–23).

So, to "be strong in the grace that is in Christ Jesus" is to live your life under the influence of the Spirit, allowing His Word to instruct and dominate your life. Paul put it this way: "Let the word of Christ richly dwell within you" (Col. 3:16). This will include a personal pursuit of holiness, confessing and repenting of all known sin, and living *Coram Deo* (that is, living in the presence of God). This was Paul's great concern for Timothy. He knew if he failed, the church would also. So he lovingly but forcefully admonished him saying, "You therefore, my son" (2 Tim. 2:1), or it could be translated "You then" or "But you my son"; as if to say, "But you, my son, unlike all the others...." I'm sure Timothy grasped the solemnity of the contrast: "You therefore, my son, be strong in the grace that is in Christ Jesus" (v. 1).

I think of this often as a pastor, and perhaps you do, as well. We live in an age where moral and doctrinal compromise in the church is considered a *virtue* rather than *high treason* against the Most High God. Tolerance of all views is touted as a virtue in keeping with the love of Jesus.

Evangelical churches that are ostensibly Christian are being swept downstream in the powerful currents of *political correctness, liberalism, feminism, egalitarianism, socialism,* and *"LGBTQism,"* to mention a few. Personal holiness and a commitment to biblical authority mean nothing to the vast majority of evangelicals. Even the message of the gospel is so distorted these days that it bears little resemblance to the true gospel of the New Testament.

Because of all this, there's always the temptation to vacillate, to equivocate, to compromise and go with the flow. Had we done that in our church, we would have outgrown our facilities years ago. But whenever I hear the criticisms, I also hear the words of the apostle Paul to Timothy, "You then, my son, be strong in the grace that is in Christ Jesus!" Or to put it more personally, "But you, David, you have been called to swim against the current, and you have the power to do so, because you are in Christ; because "[you] can do all things through Him who strengthens [you]" (Phil. 4:13). I must ask you, my reader: *Are you willing to tap into the resources that are yours in Christ and make a stand for Him?*

Dare to Be a Daniel

A dear old pastor and friend—an immigrant from Turkey—counseled me as a young man during a very difficult season in my life where I was tempted to compromise. The Ottoman government in Turkey had murdered his family (who were devout Christians) during the mass extermination of the ethnic Armenians between 1914 and 1923, a genocide known as the Armenian Holocaust. So he was well familiar with the high cost of discipleship and what was required to stand firm in the face of fierce opposition and death. I will never forget the day when he leaned in close to me, placed his hands on my shoulders and said with a quivering but firm voice, "David, dare to be a Daniel! Dare to be a Daniel! And watch what God will do!"

And this was Paul's admonition to his dear son in the faith: "You therefore, my son, be strong," a present-tense verb that can be translated, "keep on being strengthened." But it is also passive, indicating that the source of his strength would not come from himself, but from something outside of him, namely, from "the grace that is in Christ Jesus" (i.e., through his continual dependence on God).

Grace—what a marvelous word! It was grace that *saved* us when we could not save ourselves. It is grace that *sanctifies* us, because we cannot make ourselves holy. And it is grace that *empowers* us to be uncompromising and bold in our service to Christ, for apart from Him we can do nothing (John 15:5). For this reason, Paul admonishes every believer to "be strong in the Lord and in the strength of His might" (Eph. 6:10), for we have no strength in ourselves. Through his encouraging words to Timothy, Paul also gives testimony to the power of God's grace:

> But the Lord stood with me and strengthened me, so that through me the proclamation might be fully accomplished, and that all the Gentiles might hear; and I was rescued out of the lion's mouth. The Lord will rescue me from every evil deed, and will bring me safely to His heavenly kingdom; to Him be the glory forever and ever. Amen.
> (2 Tim. 4:17–18)

We can be greatly encouraged to know that God will provide all the grace we will ever need to accomplish His purposes in whatever He calls us to do or endure. He not only knows the limits of our strength, but He has ordained the circumstances that expose our inadequacies so that we will be dependent upon Him and give Him glory when He proves Himself powerful on our behalf.

Abounding Grace

In the context of the cheerful giver who "sows bountifully" that he might "also reap bountifully" (2 Cor. 9:6), Paul reveals a magnificent promise regarding God's grace when he says, "God is able to make all grace abound to you, so that always having all sufficiency in everything, you may have an abundance for every good deed" (2 Cor. 9:8). And it is the power of God's grace at work within us that animates our hearts toward godliness: "For the grace of God has appeared, bringing salvation to all men, instructing us to deny ungodliness and worldly desires and to live sensibly, righteously and godly in the present age" (Titus 2:11–12).

None of us is able to maintain the necessary strength of character to be unwavering in our faith, uncompromising in our witness for Christ, and therefore able to joyfully and effectively serve Him regardless of our circumstances. Whether we're a single person, a single parent or spouse, whether it's the role we play in our career, friendships, or responsibilities of serving Christ in His church, none of us is sufficient in himself. Recognizing this himself, Paul declared, "Who is sufficient for these things?" (2 Cor. 2:16)—a question he had already answered in 1 Cor. 15:10: "But by the grace of God I am what I am, and His grace toward me did not prove vain; but I labored even more than all of them, yet not I, but the grace of God with me."

The mystery of divine empowerment for all who will humbly yield themselves to God's Word and Spirit was so overwhelming that it drove Paul to his knees in humility and supplication for the saints saying,

> For this reason I bow my knees before the Father, from whom every family in heaven and on earth derives its name, that He would grant you, according to the riches of His glory, to be strengthened with power through His Spirit in the inner man, so that Christ may dwell in your hearts through faith; *and* that you, being rooted and grounded in love, may be able to comprehend with all the saints what is the breadth and length and height and depth, and to know the love of Christ which surpasses knowledge, that you may be filled up to all the fullness of God. Now to Him who is able to do far more abundantly beyond all that we ask or think, according to the power that works within us, to Him *be* the glory in the church and in Christ Jesus to all generations forever and ever. Amen.
> (Eph. 3:14–19)

Four Persons to Emulate

Now, the appropriate question many will ask is this: "How are we to be strong in the grace which is Christ Jesus, as Paul commanded Timothy in 2 Timothy 2:1?" Anticipating this in Timothy (and by extension, all believers), the inspired apostle goes on to give the answer in the following verses by describing four kinds of people whose characteristics every believer should emulate:

- The Teacher
- The Soldier
- The Athlete
- The Farmer

Here in verses 2–10 the Spirit of God will reveal to us in practical specifics how we can tap into the enabling power of God's all-sufficient grace we already possess. Timothy needed this. We all need to hear this, and we all need to manifest the virtues that characterize these individuals and make their pursuits so successful—topics we will examine in the subsequent chapters of this book.

3

The Teacher

The things which you have heard from me in the presence of many witnesses, entrust these to faithful men who will be able to teach others also.
2 TIMOTHY 2:2

If we're honest, we can all identify with Timothy's weaknesses. He was in a season of life where he was functioning in his human strength, operating in the flesh rather than in the Spirit, therefore bereft of courage to face the enemies in his church and the violent threats of Nero. As a young man he was also battling to maintain personal holiness and moral purity. He was even showing tendencies to be ashamed of the gospel. Life was hard. Resolve to stand firm in his faith was waning.

While our circumstances may vary, none of us is a stranger to these battles. With Timothy, we all need to be reminded of the amazing promise Jesus gave to His frightened disciples in Acts 1:8, "You will receive power when the Holy Spirit has come upon you," which came upon them at Pentecost. Suddenly, supernaturally, they were "clothed with power from on high" (Luke 24:49). And it is thrilling to know that this same power is available to every believer through our union with Christ, enabling us "to do exceeding abundantly above all we can ask or think, according to the power that works in [us]" (Eph. 3:20). But when we fail to access this power, the muscles of our faith will atrophy, our reverence for God and his Word will gradually disappear, other loves will replace our love for Christ, and we will become pleasers of men rather than of God.

Obviously, Paul did not want this to happen to Timothy. He wanted him to "be on the alert, stand firm in the faith, act like [a man, and] be strong" (1 Cor. 16:13) — a summary exhortation Paul gave to the Corinthians that can be paraphrased as follows:

- Be watchful for spiritual adversaries;
- Be firm in Bible doctrine;
- Be courageously mature in character and conduct;
- Be strengthened by the power of Christ.

So Paul exhorts him, saying, "You therefore, my son, be strong in the grace that is in Christ Jesus" (2 Tim. 2:1). Then he immediately instructs him concerning how he could do this. He wanted him to have a clear picture in his mind that would help him know how to avail himself of Christ's all-sufficient grace that would strengthen him in the great battle for personal holiness and truth—a lesson applicable for all believers. However, his first instruction seems odd at first glance. But upon further inspection, it makes perfect sense. He begins by saying, "The things which you have heard from me in the presence of many witnesses, entrust these to faithful men who will be able to teach others also" (v. 2).

He's essentially saying, "If you want to find strength in weakness, if you want to tap into the abundant resources already within you because you are in Christ, then *get serious about being a teacher of the Word of God*." Now, you might be thinking, "How does this apply to me? I'm not a teacher! Besides, he's talking with a young pastor who's supposed to take the things he's heard from his inspired mentor and 'entrust (that message) to faithful men who will be able to teach others also.'" To be sure, all that is true. However, when we compare this command to other passages of Scripture, we can quickly see that this verse paints with a much broader brush that spreads beyond the teaching priorities of pastoral ministry.

All Believers Must Teach

In biblical terms, every believer is to be a teacher! In Deuteronomy 6, God commanded His covenant people Israel to

> love the LORD your God with all your heart and with all your soul and with all your might. These words, which I am commanding you today, shall be on your heart. You shall teach them diligently to your sons and shall talk of them when you sit in your house and when you walk by the way and when you lie down and when you rise up.
> (Deut. 6:5–7)

Diligent teaching concerning wholehearted *love for* and *devotion to* the One true God was to be the constant subject of conversation that would gradually penetrate the hearts of their children, causing them to ask, "'What do the testimonies and the statutes and the judgments mean which the LORD our God commanded you?'" (v. 20). What follows in the text is the command to answer their questions according to a divine pattern that extols the wonders of God's deliverance, power, judgment, faithfulness, Law, goodness, and grace.

Likewise, the Great Commission was given to all believers:

> Go therefore and make disciples of all the nations, baptizing them in the name of the Father and the Son and the Holy Spirit, teaching them to observe all that I commanded you; and lo, I am with you always, even to the end of the age.
> (Matt. 28:19–20)

We are all called to make disciples through the teaching and application of the Word in whatever sphere of influence God has placed us. Parents are to bring up their children "in the discipline and instruction of the Lord" (Eph. 6:4). Mature women are to teach the young women (Titus 2:3–5). Every believer is to "proclaim Him, admonishing every man and teaching every man with all wisdom, that we may present every man complete in Christ" (Col. 1:28).

Every believer is to be about the business of "teaching and admonishing one another" (3:16). No matter who we are or how much we know, there's always someone who knows less than we do that we can instruct. All we have to do is look around us. There are thousands of ways to tell others about the riches of Christ, everything from teaching our children to posting biblical truths on social media—a refreshing change from the trivial talk and self-promoting pontifications for which we will give an account on the day of judgment (Matt. 12:36).

But notice the things we are to teach in the example of Timothy, namely, "The things which you have heard from me in the presence of many witnesses"(v. 2). What did he hear from Paul? Not the traditions or philosophies of men, not ideas he conjured up on his own, but what he received from Christ Himself. Timothy heard Paul speak *divine revelation*, consistent with Paul's own testimony: "For I would have you know, brethren, that the gospel which was preached by me is not according to man. For I neither received it from man, nor was I taught it, but I received it through a revelation of Jesus Christ" (Gal. 1:11–12). And Paul didn't hold anything back; he didn't selectively choose passages and doctrines that would be acceptable to his audience. Rather, he said of himself, "I did not shrink from declaring. . . the whole purpose of God" (Acts 20:27).

So he tells Timothy to "entrust [what you have heard from me] to faithful men who will be able to teach others also" (v. 2). The Greek verb "entrust" (*paratithēmi*) means "to set before" or "place beside." It denotes placing something valuable in safekeeping. Timothy was to entrust the revelation of God ("these things") to faithful, godly men "for safekeeping" and for "transmission to others."[15] There's a powerful lesson to be learned here.

We must never forget that *the canon of Scripture is an invaluable treasure that must be transmitted to others who will safeguard it and pass it along to others!* Aren't you thankful for the chain of truth that has remained unbroken down through redemptive history that brought the gospel to you?

And oh, the riches contained in the Word of God! David speaks of this in Psalm 19 when he says,

> The law of the LORD is perfect, restoring the soul;
> The testimony of the LORD is sure, making wise the simple.
> The precepts of the LORD are right, rejoicing the heart;
> The commandment of the LORD is pure, enlightening the eyes.
> The fear of the LORD is clean, enduring forever;
> The judgments of the LORD are true; they are righteous altogether.

> They are more desirable than gold, yes, than much fine gold;
> Sweeter also than honey and the drippings of the honeycomb.
> Moreover, by them Your servant is warned;
> In keeping them there is great reward.
> (vv. 7–9)

Paul expands upon the incalculable wealth contained in the Bible when he reminds Timothy that "All Scripture is inspired by God and profitable for teaching, for reproof, for correction, for training in righteousness; so that the man of God may be adequate, equipped for every good work" (2 Tim. 3:16–17). For this reason we're commanded to study it, interpret it accurately, meditate upon it, memorize it, preach it, never stand in judgment of it, and to guard it. And surely you will agree that we don't really *know* a subject until we *teach* it. We don't really *have the Word* until we *give it* away—an amazing spiritual paradox.

But this is also the key to finding strength in weakness. Why? Because this is the process the Spirit uses to produce holiness, which is essential to spiritual power over sin. We see this in the words of the psalmist: "Your word I have treasured in my heart, that I may not sin against You" (Ps. 119:11). Likewise, Paul reminded the church at Thessalonica of what produced holiness in them when he says, "For this reason we also constantly thank God that when you received the word of God which you heard from us, you accepted *it* not *as* the word of men, but *for* what it really is, the word of God, *which also performs its work in you who believe*" (1 Thess. 2:13; emphasis mine). John indicated the same when he said, "I have written to you, young men, because you are strong, and the word of God abides in you, and you have overcome the evil one" (1 John 2:14).

So Paul is essentially saying to Timothy, "My son, if you expect to be strong in the Lord, you need to be a man devoted to the apostolic message I have entrusted to you—having received it from the Lord Jesus Himself—so that you can entrust it to others!"

A Point of Distinction

It is important to note, however, that Timothy was not to entrust the sacred truths to just anyone. Instead, he was to make it a priority to consign the apostolic message to "faithful" men for safekeeping (2 Tim. 2:2). The Greek word "faithful" (*pistois*) means "trustworthy" or "dependable." Given the proliferation of heretics that were plaguing the church at Ephesus, it was crucial for Timothy to be very selective in whom he entrusted the sacred truths. Like the current state of modern evangelicalism, Timothy was dealing with some who had "gone astray from the truth" (v. 18), laypersons and leaders alike who were in opposition to the truth (v. 25; 3:8), and some refusing to endure sound doctrine to the point of turning from the truth and turning aside to myths (4:3–4).

So Timothy needed to teach faithful men who were "servants of Christ, and stewards of the mysteries of God. In this case, moreover, it is required of stewards that one be found trustworthy" (1 Cor. 4:1–2). Indeed, "the overseer must be above reproach as God's steward" (Titus 1:7). Additionally, because of his unique role as a pastor, he was to make it a priority to "entrust these to faithful men who will be *able to teach others also*" (2 Tim. 2:2, emphasis mine). While he taught everyone in his care (consistent with the public ministry of Christ and the apostles), his priority was to invest in faithful men who had the gift of teaching—a gift not everyone has. He needed to find men who would "work hard at preaching and teaching" (1 Tim. 5:17); men capable of "holding fast the faithful word which is in accordance with the teaching, that he may be able both to exhort in sound doctrine and to refute those who contradict" (Titus 1:9).

It's as though Paul is saying, "Timothy, you need to train a *Seal Team 6* to serve with you, godly men you can count on and who can train others also. Otherwise, you will never survive. Make this a priority for the glory of Christ. If you want to 'be strong in the Lord,' surround yourself with faithful men and teach them what I have taught you." Failure in this realm is why there are so many weak churches filled with weak Christians.

While the conditions in which we live are not this bleak, persecution is mounting and many Christians are already compromising morally and doctrinally, seeking the approval of men rather than God (Gal. 1:10), and joining churches that are little more than carnivals of cultural acceptance rather than "the church of the living God the pillar and support of the truth" (1 Tim. 1:15). When this happens, the following patterns will define the attitude of a wayward heart:

- Your commitment to personal holiness will diminish.
- Your love for the world will eclipse your love for the truth.
- Your prayers will be lazy, formal, self-centered, and infrequent.
- You will have no enjoyment of God in the inner

person.
- You will pant after things that are eternally inconsequential and not pant after God.
- Your commitment to serving Christ will drift into a state of lethargy, formalism, and hypocrisy.
- Your burden for the lost and zeal for evangelism will disappear.
- Eventually, you will have no real love for Christ and no longing to experience more of His power and presence in your life.

This was Paul's concern for Timothy, the saints at Ephesus, and by extension, for all believers. This is an admonition that extends to all believers. God blesses us, empowers us, and strengthens us when we devote ourselves to evangelism and discipleship as part of a team of teachers who are dedicated and determined to fulfill the Great Commission we have been given. Show me a man or woman who is weak in Bible doctrine and indifferent about teaching it to others, and I'll show you a pathetic, powerless Christian who knows little of "the mind of Christ" (1 Cor. 2:16), cares little to advance His glory, and enjoys little of His power and presence in his or her life.

Like the travelers to Emmaus who enjoyed the

company of Christ for just a short while, it is the Word of Christ that feeds the flame of intimate fellowship with Him and causes our hearts to burn within us (Luke 24:32) with such fervor that we cannot help but speak of Him. And in so doing, the power of Christ consumes us and flows through us to others. So indeed, a strong believer will be a diligent student of Scripture who is also devoted to training others and who will in turn pass the truth on to the next generation. This is what unleashes the power of Christ through His indwelling Spirit, for "if we live in the Spirit, let us also walk in the Spirit" (Gal. 5:25).

The Need for Teamwork

In January of 1925, a diphtheria epidemic broke out among the Alaska Natives around the remote little town of Nome, Alaska (then about 1,700 in population). In desperation, they contacted Anchorage for the delivery of a life-saving serum by airplane, but a massive territory-wide blizzard with winds up to eighty miles per hour and temperatures as low as fifty below zero made that impossible. The only way to get the life-saving serum was to ship it by rail to Nenana—the last railhead in Alaska—and then retrieve it by dog sled.

So they organized a relay of dog sled teams to make the 674-mile trek from Nenana to Nome.

Twenty mushers volunteered for the dangerous journey. Each man risked his life to be a part of relay that would save many lives—a relay that took seven days after the serum left Nenana. You may recall the story of the small, heroic Siberian Husky named Togo and his owner Leonhard Seppala, considered to be the greatest of all sled dog racers. Togo, the lead dog of Seppala's team, led his team to travel the furthest in the run for a total of 260 miles—a run that so exhausted Togo that it ended his racing career. Thanks to these heroic men, the inhabitants of the town of Nome were saved from extinction.

What a picture of the dedication and teamwork needed to deliver a far more precious serum—*the gospel of Jesus Christ.* And every believer is to be part of that relay team. This is what Paul had in mind when he instructed Timothy. To paraphrase his admonition in the context of this analogy, in essence Paul was saying, "Yes, the conditions are dangerous, but the need for the gospel to be delivered to men and women dying in their sins is a mission of inestimable importance—the eternal destiny of men's souls. Timothy, the Lord needs you, and He will empower you, but you must also entrust this life-saving message to other men who can be trusted to run their leg of the relay."

Teaching (discipleship) is such a wonderful expression of fellowship within the church. What a joy it is to see others grow in the grace and knowledge of Christ. And what an encouragement it is to labor together with others committed to the same, not only through formal teaching venues, but also through casual conversation. Are we not all drawn to those whose speech leads us to thoughts of God? Do we not all find ourselves personally convicted by godly friends who take seriously Paul's sober command: "Let no unwholesome word proceed from your mouth, but only such *a word* as is good for edification according to the need *of the moment,* so that it will give grace to those who hear" (Eph. 4:29).

I would humbly ask you, my reader, if you are a faithful storehouse capable of safeguarding the apostolic message of divine truth? Are you committed to knowing it and teaching it? Or do you merely feed upon the words of others with no interest in feeding anyone else?

If this describes you, then you *are* and will *remain* a weak, ineffective, vacillating Christian who knows nothing of what it means to be strong in the grace that is in Christ Jesus. You have lapsed into a state of spiritual complacency and shallowness that will render you ineffective in service to Christ. You have fallen asleep in the garden instead of "watching and praying, that you may not enter into temptation; the spirit is willing, but the flesh is weak" (Matt. 26:41). Because of this, you will forfeit blessing in your life. And when the blizzard winds of discouragement, disappointment, and persecution begin to howl, you will cower in fear, tremble in despair, and be of no help to anyone.

May we all "be strong in the grace that is in Christ Jesus," knowing that we first access the power of Christ by taking seriously the command to be a teacher who teaches others.

4

The Soldier

Suffer hardship with me, as a good soldier of Christ Jesus.
2 Timothy 2:3

After the admonition to adopt the identity of a teacher, the second kind of person whose characteristics we should emulate, if we want to tap into the enabling power of God's all-sufficient grace, is that of the *soldier*. This is a familiar and fitting military metaphor the apostle Paul uses in his epistles as a picture of spiritual strength. He implores Timothy in this regard, saying, "Suffer hardship with me, as a good soldier of Christ Jesus. No soldier in active service entangles himself in the affairs of everyday life, so that he may please the one who enlisted him as a soldier" (2 Tim. 2:3–4).

Like all believers, Timothy needed to be reminded that he was at war. War requires good soldiers who are willing to suffer whatever it takes to accomplish their mission and gain the victory. In this context, the primary enemy is *Satan* and those who serve him as opponents of Christ and His gospel, although the *flesh* and the *world* are also fierce enemies that must be vanquished. Earlier in his first letter, he charged Timothy to "fight the good fight, keeping faith and a good conscience, which some have rejected and suffered shipwreck in regard to their faith" (1 Tim. 1:18–19).

We see a similar call to arms in Ephesians 6:10: "Be strong in the Lord and in the strength of His might. Put on the full armor of God, so that you will be able to stand firm against the schemes of the devil." Every Christian must join the fight. In fact, every Christian is under attack whether he realizes it or not. And what greater rallying cry than to be told that our strength is in the Lord and not in ourselves, and that His almighty power is at our disposal. In his profound work entitled *The Christian In Complete Armour: A Treatise of the Saints' War Against the Devil*, English Puritan preacher and author William Gurnall (1616–1679) writes:

> "To be strong in the power of the Lord's might," implies two acts of faith. *First*, a

settled firm persuasion that the Lord is almighty in power. "Be strong in the power of his might," that is, be strongly rooted in your faith, concerning this one foundation truth, that God is almighty. *Second*, it implies a further act of faith, not only to believe that God is almighty, but also that this almighty power of God is engaged for its defence; so as to bear up in the midst of all trials and temptations undauntedly, leaning on the arm of God Almighty, as if it were his own strength.[16]

This was the reminder Timothy needed in order to "suffer hardship. . . as a good soldier of Christ Jesus" (2 Tim. 2:3). This is a reminder the church needs today! Too many Christians are oblivious not only to the ingenious schemes of Satan that seek their ruin, but also the formidable foe of their own flesh that so lusts after the things of the world that it grows hard toward the things of God. Look no further than the superficial content of most preaching, or the shallow substance of most prayers, and it will be abundantly clear that very few see the subtle stratagems of Satan that endanger them.

It is not at all uncommon for me as a pastor to be called into a crisis-counseling scenario where an individual, a church, a marriage, or an entire family have been totally decimated by sin. While heart wrenching, it is even more distressing to learn of the utter indifference they had toward all the forces amassed against them. Hypocrisy, worldliness, doctrinal indifference and error, spiritual apathy, prayerlessness, moral compromise, a waning love for Christ, and a basic opposition to holiness left them vulnerable to the crafty deceptions of the Serpent.

Typically complacency, a lack of spiritual discernment, and willful biblical ignorance mark the lives of weak Christians who know nothing of what it is to "suffer hardship. . . as a good soldier of Christ Jesus" (2 Tim. 2:3). Even at the writing of this book there are professing Christians whose minds are so programmed by evil that they are willing to consider a radical socialist and a homosexual to be the next president of our country. The calloused deadness of a seared conscience is so severe that many so-called Christians who are ostensibly evangelical have no problem embracing a political party that advocates for the killing of unwanted babies and proudly celebrates forms of immorality that God considers abominations.

While there is no biblical basis to validate their claim to genuine saving faith, if perchance some are merely naïve, ignorant, temporarily deceived yet truly redeemed, then they certainly know nothing of what it is to "be strong in the Lord and in the power of His might" (Eph. 6:10), nothing of wearing the full armor of God (v. 11), nothing of struggling against the rulers, against the powers, against the world forces of this darkness, against the spiritual forces of wickedness in the heavenly places" (v. 12), nothing of the weapons of our warfare not being fleshly but supernatural, able to pull down satanic fortresses (2 Cor. 10:3–4), and nothing of their need to "[take] every thought captive to the obedience of Christ" (v. 5). Yet these are the repeated warnings and resources revealed in Scripture.

The Good Soldier

Tapping into the spiritual powers of the indwelling Christ requires more than just a willingness to be a mere soldier. We must be willing to "suffer hardship" (literally: "to suffer together with someone") "as a good" (Greek: *kalos*, meaning commendable, or exceptional) "soldier of Christ Jesus." There are good soldiers and mediocre soldiers. Good soldiers are "all in" to serve their commanding officer, willing to do whatever it takes to accomplish their mission. They are willing to sacrifice everything—even their life—for a cause much greater than self-interest.

Then there are mediocre soldiers who merely wear the uniform and reluctantly answer the call of duty. They're *self-serving*, not *self-sacrificing*. They are the fair-weather, cowardly, country-club Christians whose only fight is against anyone who challenges their carnality or opposes their pet preferences.

A highly decorated, battle-scarred soldier who had just recently retired from the Army after many years of deployment told me something quite interesting. He described how an increasing number of new recruits were nothing more than "sissy boy snowflakes who are lazy, entitled, undisciplined, unsubmissive, and disrespectful." He said, "I'm sick and tired of having to deal with them!" Sadly, many professing Christians could be characterized in similar terms when it comes to spiritual warfare, and many churches cater to their needs.

Please understand: *There's a war going on!* Satan is the ever-active "ruler of this world" (John 12:31; 14:3; 16:11), the unrivaled master of disguise (Greek: *metaschēmatizō*, 2 Cor. 11:13–15) who strategizes (Greek: *noēma*, 2 Cor. 2:11; 11:3) as a master tactician (Greek: *methodeia*, Eph. 6:11); who excels at deceiving and entrapping (Greek: *planaō*, Rev. 12:9; 20:8; *pagis*, 1 Tim. 3:7; 2 Tim. 2:26) and who "prowls around like a roaring lion, seeking someone to devour" (1 Peter 5:8).[17] He is determined to defeat you, destroy your marriage, your children, your family, your testimony, and render you useless for the cause of Christ. His victims lie dead all around us.

> He tells lies (John 8:44); he influences people to lie (Acts 5:3); he disguises himself as an angel of light (2 Cor. 11:13–15); he snatches the gospel from unbelieving hearts (Matt. 13:19; Mark 4:15; Luke 8:12); he holds unbelievers under his power (Eph. 2:2; 1 John 3:8–10; 5:19); he traps and deceives unbelievers, holding them captive to do his will (2 Tim. 2:26); he tempts believers to sin (1 Cor. 7:5; Eph, 4:27); he seeks to deceive the children of God (2 Cor. 11:3); he takes advantage of believers (2 Cor. 2:11); he seeks to destroy the faith of believers (Luke 22:31); he torments the servants of God (2 Cor. 12:7); he thwarts the progress of ministry (1 Thess. 2:18); and he wages war against the church (Eph. 6:11–17).[18]

A good soldier of Jesus Christ will go to war with this evil wherever he finds it, *even in his own heart*. And there are myriads of worldly enticements and secret idols that are seemingly irresistible to our fallen nature. But because our heart is so deceitful, we can justify the most deadly poisons and we're often blind to the gravest dangers—like the unsupervised Internet access for children. I'm convinced that the cell phone is Satan's most effective Trojan Horse that he uses to infiltrate our mind with lies and to seduce our heart to sin. Yet this little device has become an idol held in virtually every hand.

While the list of temptations in our war against Satan and the flesh are myriad, the real question is this: Are you at war with sin, vigilant to the Serpent's designs to draw you into it? Are you willing to suffer hardship with others as a good soldier of Christ Jesus in taking a stand against these things, especially in your heart? Is it your ambition to please the Supreme Commander, come what may?

Avoiding Trivial Pursuits

In his attempt to strengthen Timothy in the fight, Paul goes on to instruct him saying, "No soldier in active service entangles himself in the affairs of everyday life, so that he may please the one who enlisted him as a soldier" (2 Tim. 2:4). The term "entangles" is the passive form of *emplekō* which means, "to weave," "to entwine," or "to be hindered," like being intertwined or tangled up in a line. The apostle's illustration is clear: *good soldiers don't get themselves tangled up in civilian affairs whether good or bad.*

They separate themselves from extraneous interests and trivial pursuits that might distract them from their dangerous duties. The implication for Timothy, and for every believer, is to avoid getting tangled up in things that might hinder a single-minded devotion to Christ, and stay alert and prepared to engage the enemies of our soul. Paul warns, "But I am afraid that, as the serpent deceived Eve by his craftiness, your minds will be led astray from the simplicity and purity *of devotion* to Christ" (2 Cor. 11:3).

Since I am pastor of a church near a large military base, I am privileged to know and to shepherd many soldiers. One who lives close to me is in a branch of the Special Forces, and he's a living illustration of what it means to avoid being tangled up in matters that might prevent him from effectively serving his commanding officer. He is always running to stay in shape, constantly lifting weights, training at the gun range, and training in other ways that I'm not aware of. He's dedicated—always on duty, 24/7, prepared to risk his life for others. In keeping with Paul's analogy, he wants to please his commanding officer, and stay alive!

Only when Christ is our greatest joy and most fervent love, will we "have as our ambition. . . to be pleasing to Him" (2 Cor. 5:9; 1 Thess. 2:4). We will not be a man-pleaser but a God-pleaser, ever faithful to do His will. In light of this Paul said, "If I were still trying to please men, I would not be a bond-servant of Christ" (Gal. 1:10). When we try to please the world, we will become like the world. We will drift into a fool's paradise and allow the world to shape us into its image, the very opposite of the warning in Romans 12:2, not to "be conformed to the world, but be transformed by the renewing of your mind." We will increasingly think like, look like, and act like those who hate Christ. Even though we may hold to sound doctrine, we end up forsaking our first love for Christ, like the saints of Ephesus gradually did (Rev. 2:2–4).

Fight the Good Fight

Paul wanted Timothy to be the kind of soldier that was willing to "fight the good fight" (1 Tim. 1:18), as he was willing to do. Because of this, at the close of his life he was able to say, "I have fought the good fight" (4:7). And can there be a nobler, more virtuous fight than doing battle against the kingdom of darkness to rescue the souls of men and women for the glory of God? I think not. And Paul knew that, without this mindset, Timothy would never be strong in the Lord. Unless he saw himself as a soldier engaged in fierce combat in a war whose victory is certain, he would never find strength in weakness.

Unfortunately, many believers are like soldiers who are AWOL. In fact, they don't even know they're supposed to be in active duty. They show up on Sunday mornings out of cultural tradition. They think to themselves, "It's no big deal if I'm faithful or not. Church and serving Christ is optional." For thousands or professing Christians, the church they attend is really little more than a country club where you go to socialize—a place with lots of fun things for the kids to do while the adults hang out, engage in small talk, and network their business. In fact, this is what most people seem to look for in a church.

But the mindset of a good soldier willing to suffer for Christ is radically different. Because such people have been engaged in spiritual warfare all week, they come to church out of *desperation*, not *obligation*. Worshipping their Lord, fellowshipping with fellow soldiers, and being strengthened by the nourishing truths of God's Word is a matter of life and death for them.

They've been "suffering hardship. . . as a good soldier of Christ Jesus." All week they have taken unpopular stands, posted unpopular posts on social media, and stood up to ungodly people—often in their own family. They're fatigued, wounded, and often lonely. They can identify with Jesus who was "despised and forsaken of men, a man of sorrows acquainted with grief" (Isa. 53:3). They've been proclaiming and living the truth, and most people hate them because of it. Charles Spurgeon said it well,

> The soldier is full often a suffering man; there are wounds, there are toils, there are frequent stays in the hospitals—there may be ghastly cuts which let the soul out with the blood. Such the Christian soldier must be ready to suffer, enduring hardship, not looking for pleasure of a worldly kind in this life, but counting it his pleasure to renounce his pleasure for Christ's sake.[19]

You could say the Christian soldier suffers from a spiritual version of PTSD that might be labeled: PHYSICALLY TRAUMATIZED BY SPIRITUAL DARKNESS. But he fights on for the Lord he loves. Having a living hope he sees an "inheritance which is imperishable and undefiled and will not fade away, reserved in heaven for [him]" (1 Peter 3:4). The fierce conflict only increases his craving for the glory and greatness of God and the triumph of his Majesty, the King of glory.

And as he longs for the soul-satisfying, life-giving truths of his King's instructions and promises, you can hear him say with the psalmist, "As the deer pants after the water brooks, so my soul pants after you, O God" (Ps. 42:1). Every day he dons the whole armor of God. Every day he marches on his knees in prayer and wields the sword of the Spirit with its supernatural power to destroy fortresses of evil. But in his weakness, he experiences strength. And with the apostle Paul, he affirms that God "is able to do far more abundantly beyond all that we ask or think, according to the power that works within us" (Eph. 3:20).

5

The Athlete

Also if anyone competes as an athlete, he does not win the prize unless he competes according to the rules.
2 TIMOTHY 2:4

Once again it is important to remember the context of Paul's exhortations to Timothy. Paul was aware of Timothy's weaknesses and therefore his need to "be strong in the grace that is in Christ Jesus" (2 Tim. 2:1). Moreover, because of increased Roman persecution, Paul lamented, "all who are in Asia turned away from me" (1:15). He also warned Timothy to "avoid worldly *and* empty chatter, for it will lead to further ungodliness, and their talk will spread like gangrene" (2:16), a reference to "men who have gone astray from the truth" (v. 18). Naturally, the dangerous consequences of all this is not only a departure from gospel truth, but from godliness itself. This can be seen in the shocking catalogue of personal ungodliness Paul lists in chapter 3:1–8:

> But realize this, that in the last days difficult times will come. For men will be lovers of self, lovers of money, boastful, arrogant, revilers, disobedient to parents, ungrateful, unholy, unloving, irreconcilable, malicious gossips, without self-control, brutal, haters of good, treacherous, reckless, conceited, lovers of pleasure rather than lovers of God, holding to a form of godliness, although they have denied its power; avoid such men as these. For among them are those who enter into households and captivate weak women weighed down with sins, led on by various impulses, always learning and never able to come to the knowledge of the truth. Just as Jannes and Jambres opposed Moses, so these men also oppose the truth, men of depraved mind, rejected in regard to the faith.

Obviously, in light of the grave dangers associated with Timothy's personal inadequacies and the Satanic forces raised up against the church in that day, it was crucial for him to know how to derive his strength from the grace that is in Christ Jesus and not himself. Paul knew this by personal experience as evidenced in his testimony recorded in 1 Corinthians 15:10 where he states, "But by the grace of God I am what I am, and His grace toward me did not prove vain; but I labored even more than all of them, yet not I, but the grace of God with me." Indeed, as James reminds us, "He gives a greater grace. Therefore it says, 'God is opposed to the proud, but gives grace to the humble.' Submit therefore to God. Resist the devil and he will flee from you. Draw near to God and He will draw near to you."

But we must remember: *while we can all rejoice in the all-sufficient and all-powerful grace that is ours through our union with Christ, it can only be unleashed when we function consistently with the illustrative metaphors Paul employs: the teacher, the soldier, the athlete, and the farmer*. And it's to the figure of the athlete that we now direct our attention.

Striving To Win

The man who wishes to be strong in the grace which is his in Christ must see himself not only engaged in a war like a soldier, but in a sporting competition as an athlete. To this end Paul writes,

"Also if anyone competes as an athlete, he does not win the prize unless he competes according to the rules" (2 Tim. 2:5). The term "competes" translates the Greek verb *athleō* from which we get our English word athlete. It means to compete for something, to engage in a contest, to contend, wrestle, and struggle. In describing one of the characteristics of worthy conduct in Philippians 1:27, Paul used the same term in a compound Greek word, *sunathleō*, translated "striving together"; the preposition *sun* (with) and the noun *athleō* means to compete in a contest. In both passages, the term accomplishes its purpose in conjuring up the powerful image of a highly disciplined athlete exerting every fiber of his being to excel in his event.

The saints of that day would have understood this clearly. The Isthmian games were held near Corinth every two years in honor of Poseidon at Isthmus Sanctuary while the Olympic Games where held every four years in honor of Zeus in the sacred site of Olympia. Champions were considered blessed by the gods and received special privileges over the course of their lives. Given the enormous benefits of victory, athletes were highly motivated to do whatever it took to gain the victor's wreath, which was merely a garland made at first from plastered pine leaves, although perhaps later from "celery."[20]

Everyone knows an athlete must be highly disciplined and determined to be the very best he can be to win the prize. To compete as an athlete in that day, as well as today, required enormous devotion, persistence, self-sacrifice, and self-denial. Training regimens and diet restrictions were crucial. It also required strict adherence to the rules of the competition.

I've counseled a number of professional athletes and several Olympic medalists over the course of my ministry, and I've always been fascinated to learn about their rigorous training programs.

I read where the NBA star, Stephen Curry (a 6'3" guard who plays for the Golden State Warriors) does running and dribbling drills anywhere from 2–4 hours a day and he shoots until he *makes* 500 3-pointers every day. Not only that; he also shoots 100 3-pointers before every game. No wonder he makes over $40,000,000 per year!

Not only does a serious athlete train hard, but he also maintains a highly disciplined diet. For example, the professional athletes I know will say to the man that soft drinks, sugar, processed foods (especially junk food) are like poison to their system. One professional basketball player told me, "I can't remember the last time I drank a soda, or even ate at a fast-food joint." The point to all this is simply this:

If you want something badly enough, you'll do whatever it takes to achieve it. And this was what Paul wanted Timothy to remember regarding the disciplines of the Christian life. The supernatural grace that was his in Christ Jesus was only accessible to him if he had the determination and persistence of an athlete—a lesson every Christian must learn.

It was as if Paul were telling Timothy, "If you want to win the prize of victory over your flesh, over Satan and his world system, and over all the wicked people who serve him, you need to get serious about spiritual discipline. Learn to control what you allow in your mind, feed on the Word, control your emotions, starve your lusts, exercise your faith, establish godly priorities in your life, and stay committed to them." With this in mind, he exhorted Timothy saying, "Discipline yourself for the purpose of godliness; for bodily discipline is only of little profit, but godliness is profitable for all things, since it holds promise for the present life and also for the life to come" (1 Tim. 4:7–8).

Striving Lawfully

Paul also stresses that the athlete "does not win the prize unless he competes according to the rules" (2 Tim. 2:5). The KJV translation is also helpful:

"And if a man also strive for masteries, *yet* is he not crowned, except he strive lawfully." The phrase, "strive lawfully" (*athlēsē nominōs*), means to compete legitimately, according to the rules.

It is important to note that the Greek games required athletes to meet three qualifications. First, they had to prove they were a trueborn Greek. Second, they had to swear before Zeus that they had trained for at least ten months prior to the games. And third, they had to compete according to the rules of their event. In light of these requirements, John MacArthur offers a compelling comparison with the spiritual life:

> Comparable rules apply to spiritual Christians. We must be truly born again; we must be faithful in study and obedience of God's Word, in self-denial, and in prayer; and we must live according to Christ's divine standards of discipleship. The very fact that we are Christians means we have met the qualification of being born again. But the other two requirements are far from automatic and involve constant dedication and constant effort. Together they constitute spiritual discipline, which comes from the same root as "disciple" and is the foundation of spiritual maturity.

The disciplined disciple has control of his affections, his emotions, his priorities, and his objectives.[21]

Ask yourself, "Does this describe me?" If not, you will never know what it is to be "strong in the grace which is in Christ Jesus" (2 Tim. 2:1). Moreover, you will lose out on "the surpassing value of knowing Christ Jesus [your] Lord" (Phil. 3:8) and also forfeit eternal reward at the judgment seat of Christ (1 Cor. 3:12–15). Powerful Christians are godly Christians who "labor, striving according to His power, which mightily works within [them]" (Col 1:29). While God's grace is available to all, it only empowers those who are in conscious need of it (Eph. 6:10–11). A lazy Christian is a weak Christian, having no need for strength beyond his own. But a disciplined Christian who competes as an athlete against his flesh and the forces of darkness will, in desperation, cry out for strength beyond his own and echo the sentiment of the apostle Paul when he said, "Not that we are adequate in ourselves to consider anything as coming from ourselves, but our adequacy is from God" (2 Cor. 3:5).

There will be times in our life when, like Paul in Asia, we experience "affliction. . . burdened excessively, beyond our strength, so that we [despair] even of life" (2 Cor. 1:8). But we find comfort and hope knowing that "the sentence of death within ourselves" has a purpose, "that we should not trust in ourselves, but in God who raises the dead" (v. 9).

Striving in Evangelism

I often reflect upon the same athletic analogy used in Paul's testimony to the Corinthians in relation to the discipline required to be an effective and faithful evangelist. Knowing they were fans of the Isthmian games, he asked them in 1 Corinthians 9:24, "Do you not know that those who run in a race all run, but only one receives the prize?" His question was rhetorical, so they all would respond in the affirmative. He then went on to exhort them in verses 25–27 saying,

> Run in such a way that you may win. Everyone who competes in the games exercises self-control in all things. They then do it to receive a perishable wreath, but we an imperishable. Therefore I run in such a way, as not without aim; I box in such a way, as not beating the air; but I discipline my body and make it my slave, so that, after I have preached to others, I myself will not be disqualified.

We will never be effective in evangelism unless we discipline ourselves to win the prize of new converts. Evangelism requires disciplined effort and utmost exertion in whatever part of the process we're in. This is implied in his statement, "Everyone who competes in the games exercises self-control in all things" (v. 25), which means, "They go into strict training" or "They exercise self-discipline in every area of life." It is interesting to note that the training regimen of the ancient Greek athletes also included rigorous exercise observed by their competitors in preparation for the games.

And to think that they did all this "to receive a perishable wreath" (v. 25)! All this work was for some plastered pine needles or celery leaves to be placed on their head and high honors from man. Yes, they were basically immortalized in the eyes of man, but they remained treasonous rebels in the eyes of God. It's really heartbreaking when you think about it. All that effort for the temporary praise of men, then you die and experience the eternal wrath of God — talk about misplaced priorities! How sad.

For this reason Paul went on to say, "They then do it to receive a perishable wreath, but we an imperishable" (v. 25). We serve the living Christ by exerting every ounce of effort to win souls to Christ. All the glory goes to Him! Yet we also know that "when the

Chief Shepherd appears, [we] will receive the unfading crown of glory" (1 Peter 5:4). Paul encouraged Timothy with the same promise he held dear to his heart when he said, "In the future there is laid up for me the crown of righteousness, which the Lord, the righteous Judge, will award to me on that day; and not only to me, but also to all who have loved His appearing" (2 Tim. 4:8), "the crown of life, which the Lord has promised to those who love Him" (James 1:12). This should animate the heart of every believer!

Paul continued with the imagery from the Games, saying, "Therefore I run in such a way, as not without aim; I box in such a way, as not beating the air" (v. 26), a reference to either shadowboxing or missing your opponent altogether. Here Paul underscores the need to be purposeful, direct, intentional, focused, and forceful in evangelism and discipleship—otherwise we're just beating the air.

Knowing the need to have mastery over his own flesh, he went on to add, "But I discipline my body and make it my slave, so that, after I have preached to others, I myself will not be disqualified" (v. 27). The term "discipline" (*hypōpiazō*) means "to beat" or "bruise"—a verb from boxing with the meaning, "give a black eye to." The point is this: *If we don't gain control over our bodily desires, they will gain control over us*. And this is especially true in Christian living! Think of all those who have preached to others, only to be disqualified because of some life-dominating sin. Like Paul, we must be serious about making our body our slave, rather than being a slave to our body.

Challenge to All Believers

Paul's loving concern for Timothy is obviously intended for all believers and can be summarized this way:

> Dear Christian, if you want to win the prize of victory over your flesh, over Satan and his diabolical world system, and over all the wicked people who serve him, you need to get serious about spiritual discipline. Get serious about your training in godliness. Expect to struggle, strain, sweat, and suffer, but keep exercising your faith. Be disciplined in your personal pursuit of holiness and nourish your mind with truth, for this is the key to finding strength in weakness. This is how you can "be strong in the grace that is in Christ Jesus." This is how you can experience the soul-satisfying joy of fellowship with the living God and spiritual strength to serve Him and endure the inevitable difficulties of life.

6

The Farmer

The hard-working farmer ought to be the first to receive his share of the crops. Consider what I say, for the Lord will give you understanding in everything.
2 TIMOTHY 2:5–6

Bear in mind once again the thrust of Paul's exhortation to young Timothy thus far. It could be paraphrased this way: "If you want to find strength in weakness, if you want to tap into the abundant resources already within you because you are in Christ, then you must get serious about being *a teacher of the Word of God*; you must get serious about being *a good soldier* who is willing to suffer and sacrifice whatever it takes to please his commanding officer, to accomplish his mission, and gain the victory; and you must get serious about the enormous devotion, persistence, self-sacrifice, and self-denial that marks an *athlete*. But now he adds one other figure to his illustrations—that of a "hard-working farmer" who "ought to be the first to receive his share of the crops" (2 Tim. 2:5).

Here again Paul underscores the need for self-sacrifice, self-determination, struggle, and persistence, if we expect to gain the reward of a bountiful harvest. But unlike the teacher, the soldier, and the athlete, the hard-working farmer toils tirelessly in obscurity. He has no thankful students to stimulate and encourage him like the teacher; no brothers in arms to embolden him in battle like the soldier, no crowd to cheer him on or teammates to motivate him like the athlete.[22] The hard-working farmer toils all alone. He is also at the complete mercy of the agencies of divine providence to provide for him the proper weather, to protect his crop from invasive weeds, insects, and many other parasites that could destroy his crop.

Moreover, he must do his work on the time clock of divinely ordained seasons and within their parameters. There are only certain windows of opportunity available to him to cultivate, to plant, to weed, and to harvest. His hours are long; his labor is hard and monotonous. Day in and day out he performs the same unrewarding routines, until the harvest. But in his lonely toil he carries on with unfailing determination knowing that if he quits, he fails. And if he fails, he and his family will starve. Though this is true, *the blessings of a bountiful harvest motivate him even more than the sorrow of starvation.*

Most of us know nothing of this kind of life, but this is certainly what Paul has in mind for Timothy, and each of us. My father was one of nine children raised on a little farm in western Kentucky along the Tennessee River during the Great Depression in the United States (1929 through the late-1930s). Often the family had nothing to eat but potatoes, corn bread, and buttermilk. His stories of the difficulties of eking out a living from the soil are not unlike those of many other farmers around the world. He often spoke about their life in those days saying, "We all knew that if we didn't work, we didn't eat." The Christian life is no different. If we do not work, we do not share in the harvest.

Unlike the Sluggard

Like the "hard-working farmer" in Paul's illustration, every believer must put forth the effort to persevere in godliness and Christian service, knowing that his exertion goes against the grain of his heart and the ways of the world. Indeed, this is part of the high cost of following Christ that must be counted

(Luke 14:28). As J.C. Ryle said,

> To be a Christian, it will cost a man the favor of the world. Considering the weight of this great cost, bold indeed must that man be, who would dare to say that we may keep our self-righteousness, our sins, our laziness and our love of the world—and yet be saved! . . . Surely a Christian should be willing to give up anything and everything which stands between him and Heaven. A religion which costs nothing, is worth nothing! A cheap, easy Christianity, without a cross will prove in the end a useless Christianity, without a crown![23]

We must see ourselves as "God's fellow workers" (1 Cor. 3:9) and remain "steadfast, immovable, always abounding in the work of the Lord, knowing that [our] toil is not *in* vain in the Lord." (1 Cor. 15:58). We must be the opposite of the "sluggard" described in Proverbs 20:4 who "does not plow after the autumn, so he begs during the harvest and has nothing" (Prov. 20:4). And as we toil—even in monotony and obscurity—God strengthens and blesses! Indeed, "The soul of the sluggard craves and gets nothing, but the soul of the diligent is made fat" (Prov. 13:4). The hard-working Christian is the "effectual doer" who "will be blessed in what he does" (James 1:25).

I fear too many Christians are weak in empowering grace because they are lazy in Christian piety and service. They have sown the seeds of money, power, and pleasure that will only produce a crop of bitter disappointment in the end. Worse yet, they have allowed the weeds of worldliness and the thistles of sin to choke out their ability to bear fruit, rendering them joyless in heart and powerless in service. Their lives and ministries can be likened to the sluggard Solomon described when he said, "I passed by the field of the sluggard and by the vineyard of the man lacking sense, and behold, it was completely overgrown with thistles; its surface was covered with nettles, and its stone wall was broken down" (Prov. 24:30); not so the "hard-working farmer" (1 Tim. 2:5) we are to emulate.

First to Share in the Harvest

Paul also encouraged Timothy in his labors by pointing to the bountiful harvest of God's vineyard of which he will be the first to share: "The hard-working farmer ought to be *the first to receive his share of the crops*" (v. 5b; emphasis mine). First-century farmers often worked collectively with others in every stage of the crop-raising and were often paid with a portion of the harvest. Obviously, "the hard-working farmer" would receive more than one who put forth little effort, and his reward would consist of the first share of the crops.

This is also the great promise made to every hard-working, and therefore grace-empowered believer who knows his "toil is not in vain in the Lord" (1 Cor. 3:9). This was certainly the heart of the apostle. He lamented to the saints in Rome over how he had been hindered from coming to them, "so that I may obtain some fruit among you also, even as among the rest of the Gentiles" (Rom. 1:13). His determined faithfulness to lead souls to Christ and edify the saints to do likewise can be seen in his message to the believers in Philippi when he said, "For to me, to live is Christ and to die is gain. But if I am to live on in the flesh, this will mean fruitful labor for me; and I do not know which to choose" (Phil. 1:21–22). Would that every believer were so motivated.

We can also be delighted to know that our tireless labor will produce three kinds of spiritual fruit:

- The soul-satisfying joy of a Spirit-led life (Gal. 5:22, 23);

- Righteous obedience (Rom. 6:22; Phil. 3:16, 17; Heb. 13:15);
- New converts (Rom. 16:5).

Furthermore, the harvest we anticipate is multifaceted. Not only are we rewarded by grace-empowered strength from the One we serve (2 Tim. 2:1), but we are also blessed with multiplied joy in our service to Christ—regardless of the hardships along the way (2 Cor. 6:10). For this reason all hard-working Christians toiling in the field of their respective ministries can join the psalmist and sing, "The LORD is my strength and my shield; my heart trusts in Him, and I am helped; therefore my heart exults, and with my song I shall thank Him" (Ps. 28:7).

The Harvest of Souls

And if this isn't reward enough, we can also rejoice knowing that our faithful witness has contributed to the harvest of souls. With the angels we can rejoice "over one sinner who repents" (Luke 15:10). As a reward for our toil in seeing sinners come to Christ, we "will shine brightly like the brightness of the expanse of heaven, and those who lead the many to righteousness, like the stars forever and ever" (Dan. 12:3). What a glorious motivation for every hard-working believer who labors to see sinners saved, knowing that the greater our witness, the greater our capacity to reflect the glory of God throughout eternity!

One day, every believer will stand before the judgment seat of God (Rom. 14:10) where our Lord Jesus will evaluate what we did for His glory over the course of our lives: "For we must all appear before the judgment seat of Christ, so that each one may be recompensed for his deeds in the body, according to what he has done, whether good or bad" (2 Cor. 5:10). There "each man's work will become evident; for the day will show it because it is *to be* revealed with fire [the fire of God's discerning judgment], and the fire itself will test the quality of each man's work. If any man's work which he has built on it remains, he will receive a reward" (1 Cor. 3:13–14).

This judgment doesn't merely adjudicate our *actions*, but our *motives* as well. There the Lord "will bring to light the things now hidden in darkness and will disclose the purposes of the heart. Then each one will receive his commendation from God" (1 Cor. 4:5). And what will be the reward? Scripture doesn't say exactly, but we get some hint of it in Luke 19:11–27 in Jesus' Kingdom parable of the Nobleman's Rewards and the Ten Minas. There we learn how Jesus will grant greater positions and more authority in His earthly Kingdom as a reward for faithful service motivated by a zeal for the glory of God, which will vary among believers. But whatever the Lord rewards as our share of the harvest, it will be glorious beyond our imagination, "For momentary, light affliction is producing for us an eternal weight of glory far beyond all comparison" (2 Cor. 4:17).

Closing Challenge

If it is your heart's desire to "be strong in the grace which is in Christ Jesus" (2 Tim. 2:1), you must commit yourself to emulating the characteristics of the four kinds of people Paul listed: the *teacher*, the *soldier*, the *athlete*, and the *farmer*. By drawing upon the existing grace within, we find strength in weakness; "For God has not given us a spirit of timidity, but of power and love and discipline" (2 Tim. 1:7).

Through divine revelation and personal experience, Paul knew the power associated with the imitation of the *teacher*, the *soldier*, the *athlete*, and the *farmer*, and therefore exhorted Timothy (and every believer) in these words: "Consider what I say, for the Lord will give you understanding in everything" (2 Tim. 2:7). When our character and conduct manifests the qualities of these individuals, the power of Christ's all-sufficient grace will be unleashed in our life, and the Lord will give us discernment and strength to face whatever comes our way. "Therefore, since we are receiving a kingdom which cannot be shaken, let us have grace, by which we may serve God acceptably with reverence and godly fear" (Heb. 12:28).

May we measure our lives according to these standards, and in so doing be able to share the testimony and blessings of the apostles, of the Field-Preachers—like Richard Cameron—and countless other faithful saints. And when our *teaching has been completed*, our *mission has been accomplished*, our *race has been run*, and *our crops await the final harvest*, may it be said of us what John Bunyan said of *Valiant-for-truth*—that noble character in his *Pilgrim's Progress*:

> After this, there was much talk in town that Valiant-for-truth had been given a summons by the same Messenger who had come to the others. He had been given this token that the summons was true: "Your pitcher is shattered at the spring."
>
> When he understood it, he called for his friends and told them about it. Then he said, "I am going to my Father's, and though I have come this far with great difficulty, I do not re-

gret any of it. I give my Sword to the one who will succeed me in my pilgrimage; I give my courage and skill to the one who can take it. My marks and scars I will carry with me to be a witness for me that I have fought the battles of the One who will now be my rewarder."

When the day had come that he must go on, many accompanied him to the riverside. As he went in, he said, "Where, O death, is your victory?" And as he went down deeper, he said, "Where, O death, is you sting?" So he went on over, and all the trumpets sounded for him on the other side.[24]

Endnotes

1 William Garden Blaikie, *The Preachers of Scotland from the Sixth to the Nineteenth Century* (T. & T. Clark, Edinburgh, 1888; reproduced by BiblioLife, LLC).

2 Ibid., 22, 23.

3 Ibid., 14.

4 Ibid., 150

5 Ibid., 156.

6 Ibid., 157.

7 Ibid., 157-58.

8 James Dodds, *The Scottish Covenanters, 1638-88* (Edmonston and Douglas, 1860, Second Edition) 268-79. (see, https://archive.org/details/fiftyyearsstrugg00dodd/page/n7

9 Jock Purves, *Fair Sunshine: Character Studies of the Scottish Covenanters* (Banner of Truth Trust, 2003), 58.

10 William Garden Blaikie, *The Preachers of Scotland from the Sixth to the Nineteenth Century* (T. & T. Clark, Edinburgh, 1888; reproduced by BiblioLife, LLC), 177.

11 *Biblical Doctrine: A Systematic Summary of Bible Truth*, John MacArthur and Richard Mayhue, General Editors (Crossway Wheaton, Illinois, 2017), 353.

12 Maurice Roberts, *The Thought of God* (Carlisle, PA: The Banner of Truth Trust, Reprinted 2013), 128–29.

13 Cornelius Tacitus, *The Annals*, 44.4, 5 (https://www.westmont.edu/~fisk/Articles/TacitusAndPlinyOnTheEarlyChristians.html)

14 John MacArthur, *The MacArthur New Testament*

Commentary: John 12–21 (Chicago, IL: Moody Publishers, 2008), 170.

15   Knight, G. W. (1992). *The Pastoral Epistles: a commentary on the Greek text* (Grand Rapids, MI; Carlisle, England: W.B. Eerdmans; Paternoster Press), 391.

16   William Gurnall, *The Christian In Complete Armour: A Treatise of the Saints' War against the Devil* (The Banner of Truth Trust), 24–25.

17   *Biblical Doctrine: A Systematic Summary of Bible Truth*, John MacArthur and Richard Mayhue, General Editors (Crossway Wheaton, Illinois, 2017), 682, 684.

18   Ibid., 682

19   Charles Spurgeon, *A Good Soldier of Jesus Christ*, Sermon No. 938, Metropolitan Tabernacle Pulpit.

20   Thiselton, A. C. *The First Epistle to the Corinthians: a commentary on the Greek text* (Grand Rapids, MI: W.B. Eerdmans, 2000), 713.

21   John MacArthur, *The MacArthur New Testament Commentary: 2 Timothy* (Chicago, IL: Moody Publishers, 1995), 46–47.

22   Ibid., 48.

23   J.C. Ryle, *Holiness: Its Nature, Hindrances, Difficulties, and Roots* (Icthus Publications, Apollo, Pennsylvania, 2017), 97.

24   John Bunyan, *The Pilgrim's Progress in the Allegory of a Dream*, Retold in Today's English by Cheryl V. Ford (Tyndale House Publishers, Inc., Wheaton, Illinois, 1991), 408–9.